Let's Look at Monarch Butterflies

Laura Hamilton Waxman

Lerner Publications
Minneapolis

Lerner Publications Company
A division of Lerner Publishing Group, Inc.
241 First Avenue North
Minneapolis, MN 55401 USA

For reading levels and more information, look up this title at www.lernerbooks.com.

Library of Congress Cataloging-in-Publication Data

Waxman, Laura Hamilton.
    Let's look at monarch butterflies / by Laura Hamilton Waxman.
        p.   cm. — (Lightning bolt books™ — Animal close-ups)
    Includes index.
    ISBN 978–0–7613–3886–4 (lib. bdg. : alk. paper)
    ISBN 978–0–7613–6280–7 (EB pdf)
    1. Monarch butterfly—Juvenile literature. I. Title.
    QL561.D3W386 2011
      595.78'9–dc22   2009038460

Manufactured in the United States of America
5 — BP — 4/15/15

Contents

Fluttering Monarchs

Swish! A colorful butterfly flutters its wings. What kind of butterfly is it? This is a monarch butterfly. A monarch butterfly is an insect.

Most insects have four wings.
A monarch's wings are orange,
black, and white.

A monarch spreads
its orange, black, and
white wings.

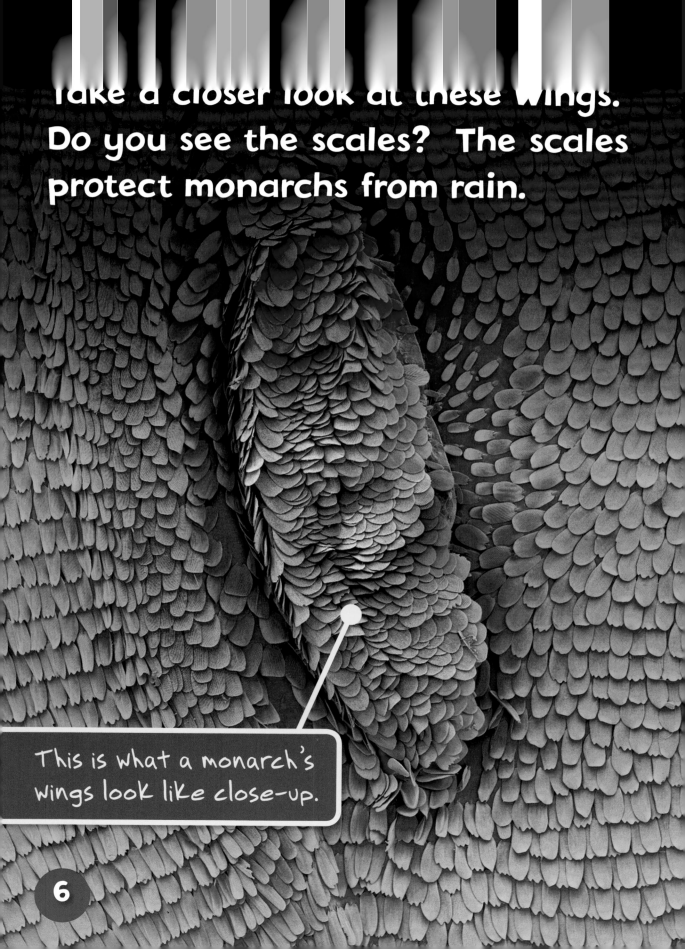

Take a closer look at these wings. Do you see the scales? The scales protect monarchs from rain.

This is what a monarch's wings look like close-up.

This monarch's legs grip on to a flower.

A monarch uses its wings to fly from flower to flower. It uses its legs to grab on to flowers.

Inside each flower is a sweet juice. **The juice is called nectar.** A monarch butterfly sucks up the nectar with its long black tongue.

A monarch draws nectar from a flower.

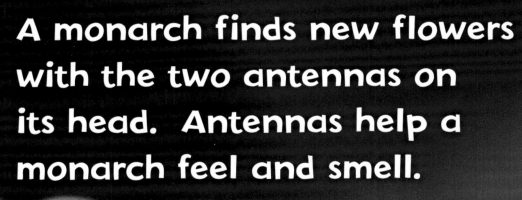

A monarch finds new flowers with the two antennas on its head. Antennas help a monarch feel and smell.

This monarch used its antennas to find a flower.

South for the Winter

In the fall, flowers die. The weather becomes too cold for monarchs. Many monarch butterflies fly south to warm Mexico.

Hundreds of monarch butterflies fly to Mexico in the winter.

The traveling monarchs sleep at night. They hang from bushes and trees.

Monarch butterflies hang from a tree in Mexico.

Hundreds of monarchs cling to the trunk of this tree. They have finally arrived in Mexico. They will rest like this all winter.

Look at all the monarchs on this tree!

Springtime

When spring comes, the monarchs return to the north. What else happens in spring?

These monarchs fly north to Canada in the spring.

Spring is the time to begin laying eggs. Female monarchs lay their eggs under the leaves of milkweed plants.

**Each egg is tiny
and sticky.**

It stays stuck to its leaf.

Look! Something is popping its head out of this egg. What is it?

An insect is hatching from this egg!

It is a monarch larva.
Butterfly larvas are also called
caterpillars.

Newly hatched monarch
larvas sit on a leaf.

Becoming a Butterfly

Monarch larvas grow bigger each day. They eat and eat. The larvas eat nothing but milkweed leaves.

A monarch larva eats away at a milkweed leaf.

A larva moves from one part of the milkweed to another.

It uses its legs to move and to hold on to the plant.

The larva keeps growing. Its skin becomes too tight. **What will it do?**

The larva molts. It wiggles out of its tight skin. Underneath is a new, bigger skin. Can you find the old skin?

A larva leaves behind its old skin after it molts.

A larva stops eating and growing after about three weeks. Then it finds a sturdy branch or twig to hang from.

The larva molts one last time.
It is becoming a chrysalis.

A monarch larva hangs from a branch. It is becoming a chrysalis.

A chrysalis hangs from a branch.

Something amazing is happening to the chrysalis. Can you guess what it is?

The chrysalis is becoming a monarch butterfly!

Out comes
the butterfly.
Its wings are
soft and wet.

Soon the wings will
harden and dry.

This new
monarch is
ready to fly!

Monarch Butterfly Diagram

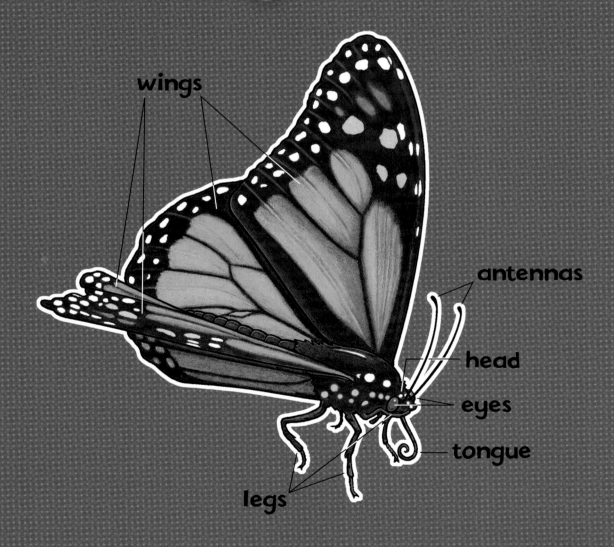

wings

antennas

head

eyes

tongue

legs

Fun Facts

- Monarchs and other types of butterflies live all over the world.

- About twenty thousand different kinds of butterflies exist.

- A butterfly's skeleton is on the outside of its body. This type of skeleton is called an exoskeleton.

- Butterflies can see red, green, and yellow.

- Butterflies taste with their feet!

Glossary

antenna: a feeler on a butterfly's head. Butterflies have two antennas.

chrysalis: the stage in a butterfly's life after it is a larva and before it is an adult. A chrysalis is covered by a hard outer shell.

insect: a small animal that has three main body parts and six legs. Most insects have four wings.

larva: a butterfly just after it has hatched from its egg. Butterfly larvas are also called caterpillars.

molt: to get rid of an old, tight skin

nectar: the sweet juice found in flowers

Further Reading

Animal Bytes: Butterfly
http://www.sandiegozoo.org/animalbytes/
t-butterfly.html

Eckart, Edana. *Monarch Butterfly*. New York: Children's Press, 2005.

Enchanted Learning: Monarch Butterfly
http://www.enchantedlearning.com/subjects/
butterfly/species/Monarch.shtml

Rustad, Martha E. H. *Butterflies*. Minneapolis: Bellwether Media, 2008.

Silverman, Buffy. *Do You Know about Insects?* Minneapolis: Lerner Publications Company, 2010.

Zemlicka, Shannon. *From Egg to Butterfly.* Minneapolis: Lerner Publications Company, 2003.

Index

Photo Acknowledgments

The images in this book are used with the permission of: © Dole/Dreamstime.com, pp. 1, 2; © Xkardoc/Dreamstime.com, p. 4; © Davidcrehner /Dreamstime.com, p. 5; © Dennis Kunkel Microscopy, Inc./Visuals Unlimited, Inc., p. 6; © Nikitu/Dreamstime. com, p. 7; © Johnandersonphoto /Dreamstime.com, p. 8; © Jim McKinley/Flickr/Getty Images, p. 9; © Richard Ellis/Getty Images, pp. 10, 12; © Richard Ellis/The Image Bank/ Getty Images, p. 11; © James Amos/National Geographic/Getty Images, p. 13; © Anthony Merciaca/Photo Researchers, Inc., p. 14; © Papilio/Alamy, p. 15; © Ron Austing, p. 16; © Lior Rubin/Peter Arnold, Inc., p. 17; © Eric Bean/Digital Vision/Getty Images, p. 18; © Ed Reschke/Peter Arnold, Inc., pp. 19, 22; © Huetter, C./Peter Arnold, Inc., p. 20; © Dwight Kuhn , p. 21; © Jeff Foott/Discovery Channel Images/Getty Images, p. 23; © Don Farrall/Lifesize/Getty Images, p. 24; © Thomas Kitchin and Victoria Hurst/All Canada Photos/Getty Images, pp. 25, 26; © Kenneystudios/ Dreamstime.com, p. 27; © Laura Westlund/Independent Picture Service, p. 28; © Musat/Dreamstime.com, p. 30; © Stevebyland/Dreamstime.com, p. 31.

Front cover: © Steve Byland/Dreamstime.com (top); © Gkapor/Dreamstime.com (bottom).

What insect has wings with orange, white, and black patterns? A monarch butterfly!

But do you know what monarchs do in the fall? Or how monarchs change throughout their lives? Read this book to find out!

LIGHTNING BOLT BOOKS™

Learn all about different animals in the **Animal Close-Ups** series—part of the Lightning Bolt Books™ collection. With high-energy designs, exciting photos, and fun text, Lightning Bolt Books™ bring nonfiction topics to life!

Animal Close-Ups

Let's Look at Armadillos
Let's Look at Bats
Let's Look at Brown Bears
Let's Look at Earthworms
Let's Look at Iguanas
Let's Look at Monarch Butterflies

Let's Look at Pigeons
Let's Look at Prairie Dogs
Let's Look at Sea Otters
Let's Look at Sharks
Let's Look at Sloths
Let's Look at Snails

LernerClassroom™
A division of Lerner Publishing Group
www.lernerbooks.com
005–008 ATOS: 3.0 Lexile: 510
Guided Reading: K

ISBN 978-0-7613-6039-1
90000

9 780761 360391

T2-DQK-443